★ IT'S MY STATE! ★

WISCONSIN

Margaret Dornfeld

Richard Hantula

Marshall Cavendish
Benchmark

New York

Other Marshall Cavendish Offices:
Marshall Cavendish International (Asia) Private Limited, 1 New Industrial Road, Singapore 536196 •
Marshall Cavendish International (Thailand) Co Ltd. 253 Asoke, 12th Flr, Sukhumvit 21 Road, Klongtoey Nua,
Wattana, Bangkok 10110, Thailand • Marshall Cavendish (Malaysia) Sdn Bhd, Times Subang, Lot 46, Subang
Hi-Tech Industrial Park, Batu Tiga, 40000 Shah Alam, Selangor Darul Ehsan, Malaysia

Marshall Cavendish is a trademark of Times Publishing Limited

All websites were available and accurate when this book was sent to press.

Library of Congress Cataloging-in-Publication Data
Dornfeld, Margaret.
        Wisconsin / Margaret Dornfeld and Richard Hantula. — 2nd ed.
            p. cm. — (It's my state!)
        Includes index.
        ISBN 978-1-60870-062-2
        1. Wisconsin—Juvenile literature. I. Hantula, Richard. II. Title.
        F581.3.D67 2011
        977.5—dc22   2010003937

Second Edition developed for Marshall Cavendish Benchmark by RJF Publishing LLC (www.RJFpublishing.com)
Series Designer, Second Edition: Tammy West/Westgraphix LLC
Editor, Second Edition: Emily Dolbear

All maps, illustrations, and graphics © Marshall Cavendish Corporation. Maps and artwork on pages 6, 40, 41, 75, and back cover by Christopher Santoro. Map and graphics on pages 8 and 39 by Westgraphix LLC. Map on page 76 by Mapping Specialists.

The photographs in this book are used by permission and through the courtesy of:
Front cover: Getty Images: Scenics of America/PhotoLink & Jonathan Kirn (inset)
Alamy: David R. Frazier Photolibrary, Inc, 9; Ilene MacDonald, 13; PhotoStockFile, 17; North Wind Picture Archives, 23, 24, 25; Nancy G Western Photography, Nancy Greifenhagen, 36; Sarah Hadley, 38; Steve Skjold, 42; Jeff Greenberg, 43, 46; Buzzshotz, 51, 53; LHB Photo, 52; GlowImages, 67; Andre Jenny, 69; PHOTOTAKE Inc, 73; . Saxon Holt, 74. **AP Images:** Darren Hauck, 47; Paul M. Walsh, 60; Morry Gash, 69. **Corbis:** Bettmann, 44. **Getty Images:** Altrendo Nature, 4; Jonathon Gale, 5 (top); Michael S. Quinton/National Geographic, 15 (bottom); Daniel J Cox, 16; Kevin Cullimore, 18 (left); Wally Eberhart, 18 (right); Frank Greenaway, 19; Armstrong Studios, 28; Popperfoto, 45 (top); Al Pereira/WireImage, 45 (bottom); Bob Rosato/Sports Illustrated, 49; Raymond Gehman/National Geographic, 50; Richard Cummins, 54; Callen Harty, 58; David Nevala Photography, 61; Scott Olson, 62, 64; Peter Cade, 70 (top); Glen Allison, 70 (bottom); Alvis Upitis, 71; Nicolas Russell, 72. **Photo Researchers, Inc.:** Tom McHugh, 5 (bottom). **Shutterstock:** Jim Vallee, 11; J. McCormick, 12; Jeffrey Stone, 14; Douglas Greenwald, 15 (top); Henryk Sadura, 57; Nancy Gill, 65. **Wisconsin Historical Society:** Image ID: 23890, 20; Image ID: 5173, 22; Image ID: 28122, 27; Image ID: 3728, 29; Image ID: 28020, 30; Image ID: 8156, 31; Image ID: 16249. 32; Image ID: 25167, 34.

Printed in Malaysia (T).
135642

CONTENTS

THE BADGER STATE

State Flower: Wood Violet

Wisconsin schoolchildren chose the wood violet as the state flower in 1909. The state legislature made it official in 1949. The wood violet has delicate purple petals. It blooms throughout the woods from March to June.

State Bird: Robin

A familiar sight in backyards, parks, and open farmland across the country, the robin is a symbol of spring. Robins sometimes nest on windowsills. They lay eggs that are a beautiful shade of blue.

State Tree: Sugar Maple

Sugar maples turn blazing gold and amber each fall. They are bursting with sap by springtime. In *Little House in the Big Woods*, author Laura Ingalls Wilder writes about her pioneer family in Wisconsin. They drilled holes in their maple trees to collect sap for making syrup.

State Animal: Badger

The badger became Wisconsin's state animal in 1957, long after the state got its nickname. People rarely see badgers because they hunt at night. When cornered, they are tough fighters, which makes them a favorite mascot for Wisconsin sports teams.

State Fish: Muskellunge

The muskellunge, or muskie, is a large, torpedo-shaped fish known for its fighting power. The largest muskie ever caught in Wisconsin waters weighed almost 70 pounds (32 kilograms).

State Beverage: Milk

The state's dairy cows produce about 10 gallons (38 liters) of milk a week per resident. Fortunately, Wisconsin citizens do not have to drink it all. Producers use about 90 percent of the milk to make cheese.

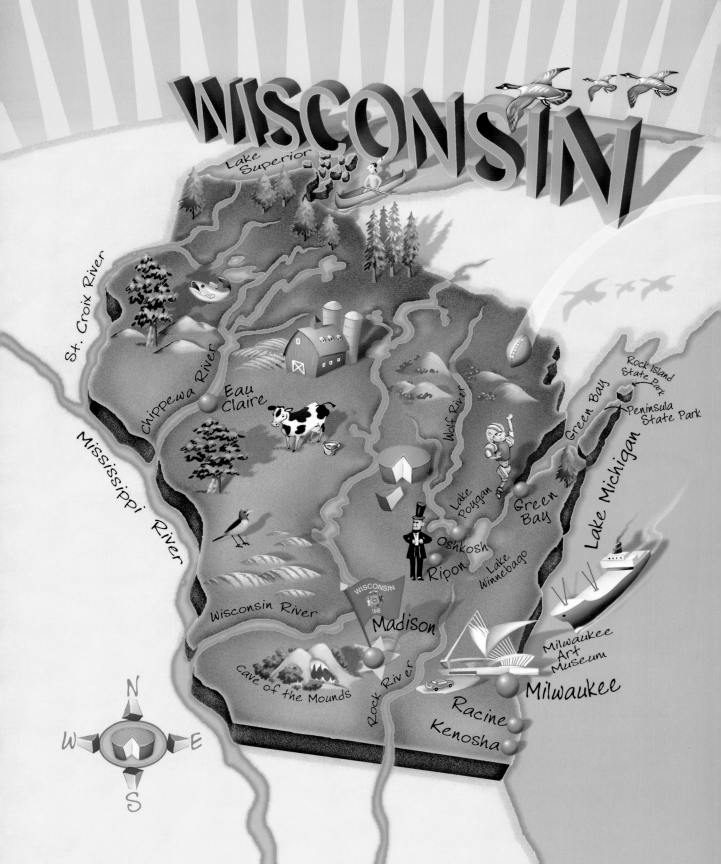

The Badger State

Many people picture simple farms when they think of Wisconsin. But it is a fair-sized place with a lot of variety. It has seventy-two counties and covers a land area of 54,310 square miles (140,663 square kilometers). Just as common as farms are woods and marshes, high cliffs and deep ravines. Some areas are crowded with towns and cities. Wisconsin has so many faces that you need time to get to know it. One way to start is to look at the landscape.

Eastern Farmlands

Many people live in the eastern part of the state. Rich soil and long, mild summers started bringing farmers to this area in the nineteenth century.

Wisconsin's biggest city, Milwaukee, sits on the shore of Lake Michigan. To the west is Kettle Moraine, a string of rolling hills with small lakes and marshes tucked in between.

Door County peninsula in northeastern Wisconsin is a thin strip of land that reaches north into Lake Michigan. Beginning in the 1800s, farmers from Belgium, Norway, and

Quick Facts

WISCONSIN BORDERS

North	Michigan Lake Superior
South	Illinois
East	Lake Michigan
West	Minnesota Iowa

Wisconsin Counties

Wisconsin has 72 counties.

Sweden moved there. Steep bluffs, sandy beaches, and cherry and apple orchards make up this narrow peninsula. Beyond its tip lies Washington Island, which many families from Iceland have made their home. Door County is known for its quiet, beautiful farmland, but its nickname tells of danger. High winds and churning waters near the mouth of Green Bay are so strong, early sailors called the area Death's Door.

Small towns dot the Fox River Valley, stretching from the middle of southern Wisconsin to the eastern town of Green Bay. Some of the state's most important mills and factories are here. The Fox flows into Lake Winnebago, the largest lake in the state, and then proceeds on to Green Bay. The world's first hydropower plant—making electricity from the energy of moving water—opened in 1882 on the Fox River near Appleton.

The North Woods

Most of northern Wisconsin is covered with forests. Leafy trees such as maple, birch, oak, and aspen mix with evergreens such as spruce and pine. Tiny lakes are tucked in the miles

Ripe cherries hang from trees in Wisconsin's Door County.

In Their Own Words

I had never been to Wisconsin, but all my life I had heard about it. . . . Why then was I unprepared for the beauty of this region, for its variety of field and hill, forest, lake?

—John Steinbeck, American novelist

APOSTLES AND LIGHTHOUSES

At the northern tip of Wisconsin lie the Apostle Islands. Along with the neighboring mainland shore, they make up the Apostle Islands National Lakeshore. This picturesque park has more lighthouses than any other U.S. national park.

of trees like hidden jewels. The Gogebic Range, extending from near Ashland into Michigan, was an important iron-mining area in the late nineteenth century and much of the twentieth century.

In the far north, hundreds of streams flow from the woods into Lake Superior. This area is known for its rust-colored rocks and tumbling waterfalls. Lake waters have hollowed out caves along their rocky shores.

Wisconsin does not have truly high mountains. Its highest point is Timms Hill in Price County in the North Woods. Timms rises 1,952 feet (595 meters) above sea level. Most of the state's big rivers, including the Wisconsin, Flambeau, Chippewa, and St. Croix, start in the North Woods and flow southwest toward the Mississippi River. The St. Croix River and the Namekagon River, which flows into it, make up the Saint Croix National Scenic Riverway, totaling 252 miles (406 km) in length.

The Driftless Area and Central Sands

During the Ice Age that ended more than ten thousand years ago, moving slabs of ice called glaciers covered much of North America. They dragged along sand and dirt, leaving behind smooth hills and ridges called glacial drift. Kettle Moraine is an example. But the glaciers never reached the southwestern part of the state. Some of Wisconsin's most dramatic scenery is in these highlands, known as the Driftless Area.

Tall buttes (mountains or hills with steep sides and flat tops) and sandstone towers seem to rise out of nowhere in the Driftless Area. A patchwork of woods and tidy farms covers its rounded hills and narrow valleys. At the Mississippi, the

Copper Falls State Park in northern Wisconsin has deep gorges, ancient lava flows, and spectacular waterfalls.

MADISON

Wisconsin's capital, Madison, is located south of the Dells. Chosen as the capital in 1836, it was named after the fourth U.S. president, James Madison, who died in June of that year. Originally founded on a narrow strip of land, or isthmus, between Lakes Mendota and Monona, the city is known for its lovely natural setting and laid-back attitude.

land suddenly plunges. The view of the mighty river from the cliffs high above can take your breath away.

In the center of the state is a swampy plain called the Central Sands. The Wisconsin River cuts through this land, shaping a narrow canyon more than 5 miles (8 km) long called the Wisconsin Dells. The river winds between rock walls that reach 100 feet (30 m) high. The water has worn them down, creating strange and beautiful forms.

The Mississippi River flows through Wisconsin's Driftless Area.

The Wisconsin Dells is a popular resort area not far from several cities.

Wisconsin Weather

Wisconsin can have brutal winters. In early December, temperatures may dive below 0 degrees Fahrenheit (–18 degrees Celsius) in the north. Lakes freeze over, wind whips the trees, and howling blizzards along the Gogebic Range can bring 3 feet (1 m) of snow. In northern Wisconsin, the wind, snow, sleet, and hail might last until May. But for most of the state, winter is not as harsh. For many, the winter weather is perfect for ice skating, skiing, and snowshoeing.

In the spring, tender buds grow on the tips of branches. As summer approaches, apple and cherry trees burst into bloom.

By July, the days are hot and muggy, but thunderstorms sometimes cool the afternoons. Some years, the state gets heavy rains that set off dangerous flooding. In 2007 and 2008, southern Wisconsin suffered record flooding, causing hundreds of millions of dollars in damage to homes and businesses. Wisconsin also experiences tornadoes, usually in the summer. The state averages about twenty-one a year. But 2005 set a record with sixty-two twisters. On August 18 of that year, twenty-seven tornadoes hit the state, a record for one day.

In the cool, crisp fall, Wisconsin's woods turn flaming red, gold, and amber. But fierce storms often batter Lake Michigan in November. The winter chill sets in again as hard rain and giant waves beat the shore.

A young girl plays outside in the snow in Wisconsin.

The prairie blazing star flower grows near the Mississippi River.

Life in the Wilds

The heavy snow and rain that fall on Wisconsin help all kinds of wild plants grow. Ferns, mosses, and delicate wildflowers such as violets, trillium, and bloodroot decorate the North Woods. Lacy morel mushrooms pop up from the ground each spring. Wild blueberries, thimbleberries, and black currants ripen each summer.

Many different kinds of orchids grow in Wisconsin. Some, such as the prairie white-fringed orchid, are very rare. Other flowers, such as bluestem and blazing star, take root in the prairies near the Mississippi River. Marsh marigolds and swamp buttercups grow in wetlands. Clinging to the windswept sand dunes of Door Peninsula in the northeast are such hard-to-find flowers as dwarf lake iris and dune goldenrod.

Wisconsin's many plants provide food for wildlife such as white-tailed deer, black bears, beavers, porcupines, woodchucks, raccoons, and snowshoe hares. Flying squirrels nibble on nuts and seeds, such as beechnuts, as they glide from tree to tree. But like many other woodland animals, they come out of their nests only at night, so they are rarely seen.

Snowshoe hare coats change from brownish in summer to pure white in winter.

Conservationists have worked to bring back gray wolf packs in Wisconsin. This gray wolf, or timber wolf, is a cub.

The fox and the bobcat are among Wisconsin's most common predators. The gray wolf nearly disappeared from the state, but conservationists moved wolves to Wisconsin from other places. Now more than six hundred roam the North Woods. Still, as of 2010, these wolves remain a federally protected species.

The lakes and rivers of the Badger State are teeming with fish such as trout, pike, perch, bass, and walleye. But the king of Wisconsin waters is the muskellunge, or muskie. This sleek, strong swimmer can grow 4 feet (1.2 m) long. It has big sharp teeth and will attack a muskrat if given the opportunity.

Wisconsin has more than three hundred types of birds, from hawks, owls, and eagles to songbirds such as blackbirds, finches, and warblers. The ever-present mourning dove is the state symbol of peace. Many waterbirds migrate back and forth along the Mississippi River. Wisconsin's Horicon Marsh echoes with the cries of these ducks, geese, swans, cranes, and herons as they stop for food along the way. Most of the marsh makes up the Horicon National Wildlife Refuge, and the rest of it is a state wildlife area.

The rare and beautiful whooping crane has not always lived in Wisconsin, but it is finding a home there now. Just a few hundred whooping cranes live in the wild. Most belong to a single flock that migrates between Texas and Canada. If food runs short or a disease spreads, all of the flock's birds could die. So to keep whooping cranes from dying out, biologists have helped to create a new flock that flies between Wisconsin and Florida.

In the summer of 2001, the scientists brought whooping crane eggs to the Necedah National Wildlife Refuge and raised the chicks themselves. They even dressed up in whooping crane costumes so the chicks would not be afraid. Cranes learn how to migrate by following their parents—so when fall came, the scientists led the way! By flying ahead of the flock in special lightweight airplanes, they got seven cranes to travel the 1,250 miles (2,000 km) to Florida. They repeated the process with more cranes in following years. Once the young cranes have made the trip south, they return north in the spring on their own. If all goes well, Wisconsin will have 125 whooping cranes by 2020.

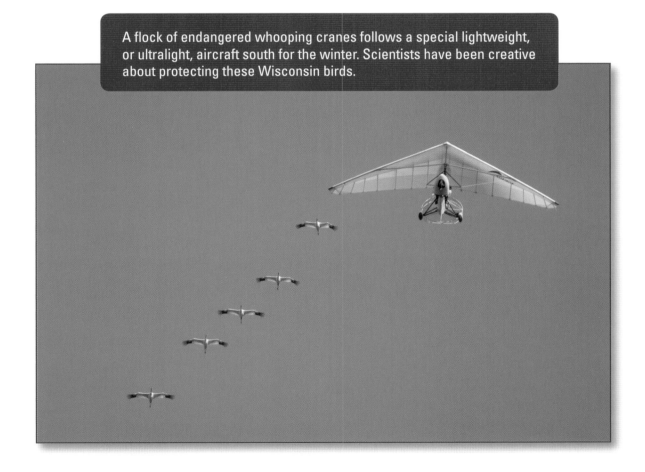

A flock of endangered whooping cranes follows a special lightweight, or ultralight, aircraft south for the winter. Scientists have been creative about protecting these Wisconsin birds.

Plants & Animals

Morel Mushroom

Many people prize morel mushrooms, often found at the base of dead trees, for their delicious flavor. But be careful—only people who know how to recognize the cone-shaped morels should collect and eat them. Other types of mushrooms can be poisonous.

Trillium

Trillium is easy to spot on the forest floor each spring. Its flowers have three large petals and can be white, purple, or pink.

Yellow Perch

Schools of yellow perch swim in Lake Michigan and the large lakes and rivers of inland Wisconsin. In the 1990s, the perch population in Lake Michigan began dropping rapidly, and restrictions were imposed on yellow perch fishing. Several years later there were signs the population might be increasing again.

Red-Winged Blackbird

Red-winged blackbirds nest in marshy areas of Wisconsin in early spring. They like to rest on cattails and defend their territory with their loud, long call, "ok-a-LEEEE."

White-Tailed Deer

White-tailed deer are common in wooded areas all over Wisconsin. They nibble young leaves, acorns, berries, and grass as well as wheat and alfalfa crops. Wisconsin has named the white-tailed deer the state wildlife animal.

Dragonfly

Dragonflies live near bodies of water in Wisconsin. But Door County is one of the few places in the United States where you'll find the Hine's emerald dragonfly, an insect as long as 3 inches (8 centimeters) with shimmering green eyes. It is endangered, which means there are so few of them, there is a risk they will die out.

From the Beginning

Here and there in southern Wisconsin, mysterious mounds can be seen. The people who made them are called Mound Builders. They began living in what is now Wisconsin more than 2,500 years ago. When seen from above, some of these mounds are long and straight. Others are shaped like animals—such as eagles, rabbits, bears, and buffalo—or people. Scholars believe that the mounds might have had some sort of religious or ceremonial purpose.

Human life in present-day Wisconsin goes back even farther. Stone tools found buried in the ground show that people were around as early as 10,000 BCE.

Many groups of people have lived in the region since the days of the Mound Builders. The Menominee and Ojibwe, or Chippewa, Indians gathered wild rice in the north. The Ho-Chunks, or Winnebagos, settled in the central region and the south. They raised corn, beans, and squash and speared fish in rivers and streams. A branch of the

Quick Facts

WISCONSIN UNDER WATER

Hundreds of millions of years ago the land that is now Wisconsin lay under a warm shallow sea. Today, across the state, you can find fossils, or remains, of small creatures called trilobites, which lived in that sea. The type of trilobite called *Calymene celebra* is the state fossil.

In this photograph from the early 1900s, an Ojibwe, or Chippewa, mother stands with her two children at Wisconsin's Lac du Flambeau Indian Reservation. She carries her infant in a cradleboard.

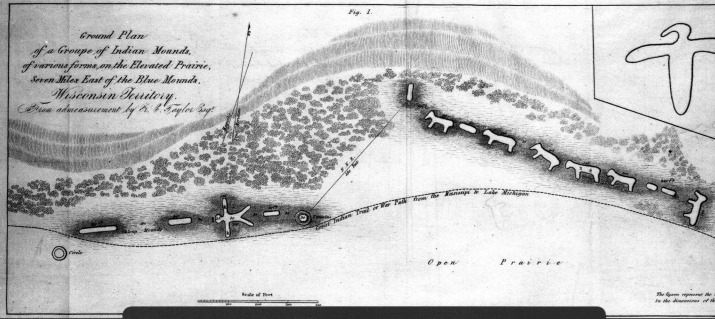

This illustrated map from 1838 shows prehistoric American Indian mounds 7 miles (11 km) east of Blue Mounds. American Indians may have created the mounds for some kind of ceremony.

Lakota tribe lived in what is now Wisconsin. The forests were also home to the Foxes, or Meskwakis, the Sauks, the Potawatamis, and the Kickapoos.

The French Arrive

French explorer Étienne Brûlé visited the area around Lake Superior in 1622 or 1623. It is not clear whether he was the first European in what is now Wisconsin. Another French explorer, Jean Nicolet, is known to have visited present-day Wisconsin in 1634. He was looking for a way to sail across North America to China so the French could buy silk there and ship it home. Nicolet landed on the shore of Green Bay, where he met a group of Indians. "He wore a grand robe of China damask, all strewn with flowers and birds of many colors," wrote a man who knew him. Nicolet was far from China, but the Wisconsin woods held their own riches.

The forests were full of muskrat, foxes, mink, and beavers, which Europeans valued for their furs. French fur traders soon made their way to Wisconsin. American Indian hunters traded their many animal skins for guns, cloth, and metal tools.

French explorer Jean Nicolet landed on the shore of Lake Michigan in present-day Wisconsin in 1634.

In 1673, two French explorers—Father Jacques Marquette (a Catholic priest) and Louis Jolliet (a fur trader)—became the first Europeans to cross present-day Wisconsin. They canoed from Green Bay as far as they could up the Fox River. Then, Indians told them where to carry their boats from the Fox to the Wisconsin River, just 1.5 miles (2.4 km) away. From there they could travel downstream to the Mississippi River. French fur traders later used this path between rivers to move between trading posts on the Great Lakes and the Mississippi.

Father Jacques Marquette and Louis Jolliet of France travel by a canoe on the Upper Mississippi River in 1673.

The Battle of Bad Axe took place in Wisconsin. It was the final battle of the Black Hawk War of 1832.

Indian Wars

Between 1754 and 1763, France and Britain fought for control of eastern North America in the French and Indian War. At the end of the war, the victorious British took control of land that included what is now Wisconsin. Twenty years later, the United States won independence from Britain in the American Revolution, and Wisconsin became U.S. land.

By the early 1800s, the fur trade was fading, and settlers now wanted to move onto the Indian lands. The U.S. government talked the region's American Indians into giving up their territory. In most cases, the natives signed official agreements called treaties with the United States. Some agreed to move west across the Mississippi River. Later on, they longed to return to their homelands.

The Black Hawk War took place in 1832 after a Sauk leader named Black Hawk helped a group of Indians return to their lands in Illinois. When U.S. troops came to remove them, the Indians fled north to Wisconsin. Black Hawk's people fought to defend themselves, but they were outnumbered. When they tried to get back over the Mississippi River, U.S. soldiers stopped them, killing many in the process.

The government let some tribes try to make a living on reservations—areas of land set aside for them. Many tribes adapted to the changing ways. Others lived in poverty among the white people, often moving from place to place in search of work and food.

Nineteenth-Century Growth

Little by little, settlers spread across the Wisconsin frontier. Many came from the East Coast, others from nearby states and territories. Some men mined lead in the southwest. Others built farms near the rivers that flowed into Green Bay. As more settlers arrived in the area, outposts such as Fort Winnebago, built in 1827, were established to make life safer for the settlers.

Wisconsin was once part of the Northwest Territory of the United States, then, in turn, the Indiana Territory, the Illinois Territory, and the Michigan Territory. In 1836, it became a territory of its own. To become a state, it needed to have at least 60,000 residents. By 1845, its population reached 155,000, but statehood also required the adoption of a constitution. In March 1848, Wisconsin voters finally approved a constitution, and two months later Wisconsin became the thirtieth state.

In the 1850s, word quickly spread that land in Wisconsin was rich and cheap. People rushed in from other parts of the country as well as from Germany, Ireland, Great Britain, Norway, Holland, Switzerland, and Belgium. Loggers cut pine from the forests and sent it down the rivers to busy sawmills. Settlers planted wheat in cleared fields. Railroads soon crisscrossed the state.

Between 1850 and 1900, Wisconsin's population swelled from about 300,000 to more than 2 million. More than 90,000 Wisconsinites took part in the Civil War from 1861 to 1865. Overall, during the second half of the nineteenth century, new industries created plenty of jobs. Factory workers made bricks, paper, machinery, and iron tools. In Milwaukee, hundreds of men and women worked in beer breweries. Quarrying—taking stone from the ground for use in making such things as roads and buildings—became a big industry. Today, red granite, which is quarried in Wisconsin, is the state rock.

Lumbering was a key industry, especially in the northern half of Wisconsin in the 1870s through the 1890s. Between 1888 and 1893, one-fourth of Wisconsinites' wages came from lumbering. Agriculture and the timber industry have contributed so much to the state that Wisconsin even has an official state soil, selected in 1983. Antigo silt loam is named after the Wisconsin city of Antigo.

Workers completed the first railroad to cross Wisconsin, from Milwaukee to Prairie du Chien, in 1857. Rail transportation contributed greatly to the Midwest's development.

RECIPE FOR CHEESE

Firm cheeses such as cheddar require special supplies, but you can make a kind of cottage cheese at home. Ask an adult to help you with the stove.

WHAT YOU NEED

2 tablespoons (30 milliliters) white vinegar

1 quart (0.9 liter) whole or 2 percent milk

1 package new cheesecloth, about 2 square yards, or 1.7 sq m (available in grocery stores)

$^1/_4$ teaspoon (1.2 grams) salt (optional)

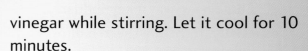

Measure 1 tablespoon (15 ml) of the vinegar into a cup and set it nearby.

Pour the milk into a pot on the stove and turn the heat to high. Stir the milk constantly. As it heats up, do not let the milk boil. When it is close to boiling, you will see very thick steam and a few tiny bubbles near the edges. Turn off the heat.

Stir vigorously as you pour in the first tablespoon (15 ml) of vinegar. Within 30 seconds, the milk should turn into curds (little blobs) and whey (clear, greenish liquid). If it does not, heat and stir it a little longer. Once you have the curds and whey, add the second tablespoon (15 ml) of

vinegar while stirring. Let it cool for 10 minutes.

While the curds and whey cool, cut the cheesecloth into three pieces that will cover a colander with only a little hanging over the sides. Lay them crisscross in the colander. Strain the curds and whey through the cheesecloth and colander and into the sink. Fold the flaps of the cheesecloth over the colander and set it on a plate in the refrigerator for an hour.

When the cheese is ready, you can add salt if you want. Be sure to refrigerate the cheese you do not eat. The next time you make cheese, try using a cider or herb vinegar. See which flavor you like best!

 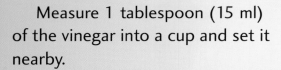

Dairy farms also spread across the state, making Wisconsin an important center for milk, butter, and cheese production.

Despite successes, the state also faced hard times. On October 8, 1871, a terrible forest fire hit northeastern Wisconsin. High winds fanned the flames into a blazing tornado that whipped the western shore of Green Bay. A large portion of six counties burned, including the entire town of Peshtigo. More than a thousand people were killed. The Peshtigo fire remains the most deadly forest fire in U.S. history.

In Their Own Words

The flames darted over the river as they did over land, the air was full of them, or rather the air itself was on fire.

—Peter Pernin, an eyewitness to the Peshtigo fire

This illustration of the Peshtigo fire appeared in *Harper's Weekly* in 1871. Some people escaped by plunging into the river.

Robert M. La Follette Sr. gives an emphatic speech in Brillion, Wisconsin, probably during the 1924 campaign.

The Wisconsin Idea

In the 1900s, a new kind of politics gripped Wisconsin. It was introduced when Robert M. La Follette Sr. was elected governor in 1900. La Follette pushed for laws to make politics and business more honest, earning him the nickname "Fighting Bob." His sons, Robert M. Jr. and Philip, became leading politicians, too.

The La Follettes saw education as the key to good government, and they helped make the University of Wisconsin one of the nation's top schools. Wisconsin became known as a progressive state willing to try new ideas. Its formula for success—getting experts to study state problems and offer advice—was called the Wisconsin Idea.

As part of Wisconsin's progressive spirit, mill and factory workers started calling for better treatment. They wanted an eight-hour workday. They also fought for a guaranteed minimum wage. In 1911, Wisconsin became one of the first states in the country to pass a workers' compensation law, granting

Wisconsin was one of the first states to support workers' rights. These female factory workers are making parts for cream separators in Milwaukee around 1918.

The Great Depression of the 1930s was a difficult time for many American families. This needy family in Madison was denied relief by the county government.

payments to people hurt on the job. In 1911, the state set up the Wisconsin Industrial Commission, which worked to ensure safe factories.

The Wisconsin Idea helped put food on the table during the Great Depression, when large numbers of people lost their jobs. In 1932, Wisconsin started the first unemployment insurance program in the United States. It gave jobless men and women money to help them get by. The state also hired people to work on major projects, such as replanting forests and building new roads.

Wars and Civil Rights

After the United States entered World War II in 1941, industries in Wisconsin, including shipbuilding and manufacturing, provided supplies for the armed forces, just as they had during World War I. The demand for war supplies created much-needed jobs for many Wisconsinites. About 120,000 served in the military in World War I (in which the United States fought from 1917 to 1918). More than 330,000 Wisconsinites served during World War II, which ended in 1945.

After the war, large numbers of African Americans from the South moved to Wisconsin. By 1960, the state had nearly 600 percent more African Americans than in 1940. These newcomers settled mainly in Milwaukee and a few other cities. They were often not allowed to live in the same areas as white people, and their children went to separate, or segregated, schools.

The U.S. Supreme Court outlawed the segregation of public schools in 1954. Cities and towns were slow to end the separation of races in public schools, however. Calls for change, giving black people the same civil rights as white people, grew louder throughout the United States.

In the 1960s, thousands of African Americans marched through the streets of Milwaukee to demand the right to live in the same areas as white residents. It was called fair, or open, housing. The state legislature passed an open-housing law in 1965, but it was rather weak. Riots in Milwaukee during the summer of 1967 left four people dead. In April 1968, the U.S. Congress enacted a fair-housing law for the entire country. Milwaukee then quickly passed its own strong

In 1967, civil rights activist and Catholic priest James Groppi leads a fair housing march down a Milwaukee sidewalk.

fair-housing law. The federal courts also forced Milwaukee to desegregate its schools, and the city began carrying out the court order in 1979.

During the 1960s, many students on college campuses in the state, especially at the University of Wisconsin in Madison, began actively opposing the Vietnam War. (Other protests occurred on campuses nationwide.) In 1970, protesters used firebombs against a university building in Madison. Some of the antiwar protesters went on to fight for other issues, such as environmental protection laws.

Important Dates

★ **c. 700 BCE** Indians called Mound Builders begin living in what is now Wisconsin.

★ **1634** French explorer Jean Nicolet becomes the first European known to have landed in today's Wisconsin.

★ **1673** Jacques Marquette and Louis Jolliet find a water route from Lake Michigan to the Mississippi River.

★ **1763** The Wisconsin region becomes British territory.

★ **1783** The land that is now Wisconsin becomes part of the United States.

★ **1804** The U.S. government and leaders of the Sauk and Fox tribes sign the Treaty of Saint Louis, in which the Indian leaders give up large areas of today's Missouri, Illinois, and Wisconsin.

★ **1829** Potawatomi, Ojibwe, Ottawa, and Ho-Chunk tribes sign the Treaty of Prairie du Chien, giving southern Wisconsin and northern Illinois lands to the U.S. government.

★ **1832** U.S. troops fight the Sauks and the Foxes in the Black Hawk War.

★ **1836** The Wisconsin Territory is established.

★ **1848** Wisconsin becomes the thirtieth U.S. state.

★ **1857** Workers complete the first railroad to cross the state, from Milwaukee to Prairie du Chien.

★ **1871** More than one thousand people die in the Peshtigo fire.

★ **1900** Robert M. La Follette Sr. is elected governor of Wisconsin.

★ **1921** Wisconsin makes discrimination against women illegal.

★ **1932** Wisconsin passes the first unemployment insurance law to help jobless workers.

★ **1993** A poisonous microbe, *Cryptosporidium*, pollutes Milwaukee's drinking water, killing dozens of people.

★ **2004** Louis J. Butler Jr. becomes the first African American to serve on Wisconsin's supreme court.

★ **2008** Wisconsin voter turnout in the U.S. presidential election (almost 73 percent) is second only to Minnesota's.

The People

Wisconsin's people come from many different backgrounds, and they are proud of their varied heritage. But the experience of living in the Badger State—braving snowstorms, working in fields or factories, listening to geese pass overhead, or watching a football game—also brings them together. In spite of their differences, Wisconsinites share many common goals and a strong sense of community.

European Roots

European families once came to Wisconsin by the thousands in search of land and political or religious freedom. Their hopes and dreams, their music and stories, help shape the state's culture today.

More than two-fifths of Wisconsin's population is at least partly of German heritage. Most German immigrants came to the state between 1845 and 1900. German Americans helped turn Milwaukee into America's leading beer-brewing city. Traditional German foods such as bratwurst,

Quick Facts

THE POLKA STATE
The polka, brought by settlers from central Europe, is the state dance. Wisconsinites play polka music on the radio, at weddings and town festivals, and even at football games.

An American Indian dancer takes a rest at an Indian Summer Festival powwow, held on Milwaukee's lakefront.

Turner Hall of Monroe is a cultural center for Swiss heritage in Wisconsin.

sauerkraut, and *schaumtorte*, a melt-in-your-mouth dessert often served with whipped cream and strawberries, are still popular all over the state.

In Milwaukee, you will find tasty Irish stew, Italian pasta, Serbian pastries, Swiss fondue, and Polish sausages called kielbasa. European traditions are alive

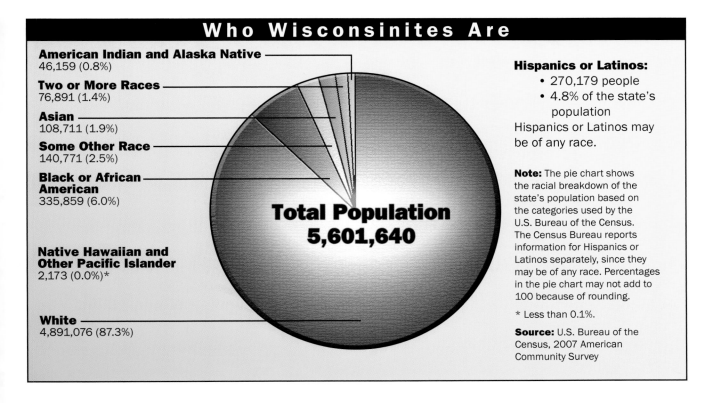

Who Wisconsinites Are

American Indian and Alaska Native
46,159 (0.8%)

Two or More Races
76,891 (1.4%)

Asian
108,711 (1.9%)

Some Other Race
140,771 (2.5%)

Black or African American
335,859 (6.0%)

Native Hawaiian and Other Pacific Islander
2,173 (0.0%)*

White
4,891,076 (87.3%)

Total Population 5,601,640

Hispanics or Latinos:
- 270,179 people
- 4.8% of the state's population

Hispanics or Latinos may be of any race.

Note: The pie chart shows the racial breakdown of the state's population based on the categories used by the U.S. Bureau of the Census. The Census Bureau reports information for Hispanics or Latinos separately, since they may be of any race. Percentages in the pie chart may not add to 100 because of rounding.

* Less than 0.1%.

Source: U.S. Bureau of the Census, 2007 American Community Survey

in other parts of the state as well. Just south of Milwaukee, in Racine, Danish bakeries make a fruit-filled coffeecake called *kringle*. Kewaunee County, in eastern Wisconsin, is known for its Czech and Belgian heritage, while in the north, family names are often Finnish. Farmers from Norway settled many towns in southern Wisconsin. On May 17, they celebrate Norway's independence day, dancing to music played on the Hardanger fiddle, a beautifully decorated Norwegian violin.

Quick Facts

LARGEST CITY
Milwaukee was formed in 1846 by combining three neighboring areas. Only about 10,000 people lived there at the time. The city grew quickly. By 1860, it had more than 45,000 residents and was one of the twenty biggest towns in the United States. Today, Milwaukee has a population of about 600,000.

MAKING A ROSEMALING DESIGN

Rosemaling is the art of painting flowers and other designs on plates and furniture. It started in parts of Norway in the 1700s. Immigrants arriving in America brought the art form with them to the upper Midwest. Settlers decorated their plates and dishes, wooden tables and chairs, storage trunks, ceilings, and walls.

WHAT YOU NEED

Sturdy white paper plate

Pencil

Paintbrush

Poster paints

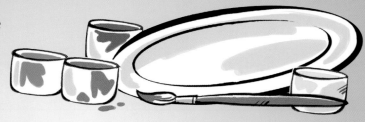

First draw your design on the plate using a pencil. There are five basic patterns—the C and backward C, the S-curve, the O, the straight line, and the dot. You can add flowers within these designs. Once you are happy with your penciled design, you can start painting.

Make the plate as bright and colorful as possible. If you want, you can use traditional colors: blue, gray, green, red, and orange for the background; white, yellow, and lighter shades of blue and green for the main designs; and yellow for outlining.

Let the paint dry before handling your plate. When it is ready, put it on display and show it to your family and friends. Try creating different designs on different plates. If you find a design that you really like, you can try it out on a small, unpainted wooden box. Craft stores sell boxes of different sizes and styles.

From Near and Far

African Americans have a long history in Wisconsin. Black fur traders worked in the area in the 1700s. In the 1800s, African Americans lived in the state's cities or built their own farming towns. In the late 1800s, the African-American community at Pleasant Ridge, near Lancaster, had its own church and school. Today, Milwaukee, Racine, and Madison have the state's largest African-American communities.

Many of Wisconsin's newest immigrants have come from Asia and Latin America. Members of a Southeast Asian group called the Hmong began

Many families have moved to the Midwestern states from Southeast Asia. These Hmong sisters watch a local parade from their steps.

moving to the state in the 1970s. Their language and culture are part of many communities. The town of Appleton, for example, is the home of a Hmong radio station. Wisconsin's Hispanic population, which more than doubled between

1990 and 2000, is still growing fast in cities such as Milwaukee, Madison, and Racine. By 2007, the state's Hispanic population was estimated to have grown 40 percent since 2000. Many Spanish-speaking families come from Mexico or Puerto Rico.

The people who have been in the region the longest are American Indians. More than 45,000 American Indians currently live in Wisconsin. Many of them call Milwaukee or Madison home, but many also return often to one of Wisconsin's eleven reservations. These lands belong to the Ojibwe, Ho-Chunk, Menominee, Oneida, Potawatomi, and Stockbridge-Munsee tribes. Throughout the year, different American Indian groups hold traditional festivals and celebrations. These special events are a way to honor their past and share their cultures with others.

Wisconsin has many native Spanish speakers, including this girl enjoying an outdoor marketplace in Kenosha.

Famous Wisconsinites

Belle Case La Follette: Social Activist

Belle Case, born in Wisconsin in 1859, was the first woman to graduate from the University of Wisconsin Law School. She married and had a family with Robert La Follette Sr. Belle Case La Follette used her education and experience to help her husband and sons during their political careers. As a respected public speaker and journalist, she worked for women's rights, opposed war, and fought for child labor reform and racial equality.

Laura Ingalls Wilder: Writer

Laura Ingalls Wilder is the author of the *Little House* books, about life on the Midwestern frontier. Born in 1867, Wilder grew up in the days of the covered wagon and became a teacher in a one-room schoolhouse when she was only fifteen. By the time she was in her sixties, the United States had completely changed. She decided to share her story of life as a pioneer girl. One of her best-loved books, *Little House in the Big Woods*, takes place in Pepin, Wisconsin, where she was born.

Frank Lloyd Wright: Architect

In the early twentieth century, Frank Lloyd Wright, born in 1867, was known around the world for his original buildings. He was famous for the striking ways he combined sleek, modern forms with light and nature. Wright believed in shaping houses to fit the land around them. One of his best-known designs is a house he built for himself called Taliesin. Shaped like a rock ledge, it juts out from a wooded hillside in Spring Green.

Harry Houdini: Magician

Ehrich Weiss was born in Budapest, Hungary, in 1874 and moved with his family to Appleton, Wisconsin, when he was four. He grew up to become one of the most amazing magicians of his time—Harry Houdini. He was best known as an escape artist. He could be handcuffed, jailed, or bound in chains, even locked in a box underwater, and somehow he would always get out. He died in 1926 on October 31.

John Bardeen: Scientist

The only person to win the Nobel Prize in physics twice, John Bardeen was born in 1908 in Madison. He went to school there and studied electrical engineering at the University of Wisconsin. Bardeen received his first Nobel Prize in 1956 for helping to invent the transistor (a device that amplifies and switches electrical signals). His second, in 1972, was for his research on superconductivity, the ability of some materials to carry, or conduct, electricity without any resistance at all.

Les Paul: Musician and Inventor

Les Paul gained fame as a guitarist, playing jazz and other types of music, including his own works. But he is also remembered for helping to develop the solid-body electric guitar and multitrack recording. Born Lester William Polfuss in 1915 in Waukesha, he played the harmonica and banjo before turning to the guitar. He was admitted to the Rock and Roll Hall of Fame in 1988 and the Inventors Hall of Fame in 2005. Paul died in 2009.

Young Wisconsinites dance at a family event at the Kenosha County Fairgrounds in Wilmot.

Taking the Lead

People have been coming to Wisconsin to start anew for hundreds of years. That might be one reason the state has a reputation for being open to new ideas. In the early 1900s, Wisconsin was one of the first states in the country to support women's rights, improvements for workers, and laws to keep big business from having too much power. In 1919, it was the first state to ratify (approve) the Nineteenth Amendment to

Quick Facts

FIRST KINDERGARTEN
In 1856, a Watertown schoolteacher, Margarethe Meyer Schurz, opened the first kindergarten in the United States. Her goal was to give young children a chance to learn and grow creatively. She had learned about kindergartens growing up in Germany. *Kindergarten* means "children's garden" in German.

the U.S. Constitution, giving women the right to vote. Two years later, it became the first state to pass a law giving women the same rights as men.

One issue facing citizens in Wisconsin today is the divide between black and white communities. In the Milwaukee area, for example, African Americans tend to live in the central city, while the suburbs have mostly white residents. In 2007, African-American males were nearly three times more likely to be out of work than white males in Milwaukee County. The schools in the central city are some of the state's most troubled. That may explain why only 68 percent of the state's black students compared to 93 percent of its white students graduated from high school in 2007.

Wisconsin is focusing on education to make things more equal. In 1990, Milwaukee became the first U.S. city to start a "school choice" program. Although a number of parents believe private schools provide a better education than

A first grader learns how to read using an online program in one of Milwaukee's south side elementary schools.

public schools, private school tuition costs too much for many families. Under the school choice program, families can get public money to send their children to private schools. The money comes in the form of a voucher—an agreement to take funds from public schools to help pay for private school educations.

At the beginning of 2009, there were 125 private schools in the program, educating nearly 20,000 students. Still, not everyone thinks school choice is a good idea. Some worry that it hurts the public educational system.

Wisconsin Sports

The Badger State is big on sports. The state's Major League Baseball team, the Brewers, is based in Milwaukee. The Milwaukee Bucks represent the state in the National Basketball Association (NBA). When football season begins, nothing gets people more excited than a Green Bay Packers game. Fans will bundle up and sit through snowstorms to watch the Packers play at icy Lambeau Field.

Outdoor sports such as boating, swimming, skiing, and snowmobiling are popular in Wisconsin. Hikers can climb portions of the U.S. North Country National Scenic Trail as well as the Ice Age Trail, a national and state scenic trail in central and southern Wisconsin more than 1,000 miles (1,600 km) long.

Hunting is another popular outdoor pastime. The favorite retriever dog of many Wisconsin hunters is the American water spaniel. One of the few breeds of dogs that originated in the United States, it was developed in Wisconsin. The American water spaniel is the state dog.

With more than 15,000 lakes in the state, many people enjoy

Quick Facts

STATE OF MUSIC
The music for Wisconsin's state song, "On, Wisconsin!" was borrowed from the University of Wisconsin football team's song. The famous bandleader and composer John Philip Sousa called that fight song the best college song he ever heard. The state also has an official ballad, "Oh Wisconsin, Land of My Dreams," and waltz, "The Wisconsin Waltz."

A Green Bay Packers fan supports his football team.

boating and fish for much of the year. Sturgeon fishing on Lake Winnebago, however, is allowed only for a short time in February. The ice at that time is usually like a layer of thick rock, and the temperature may drop to –20 °F (–29 °C). But hearty anglers say the thrill of cutting a hole in the ice and spearing one of these monsters is worth it. Sturgeon can grow 6 feet (1.8 m) long, weigh up to 80 pounds (36 kg) or more, and live as long as 150 years.

Wisconsinites appreciate many water sports, such as kayaking at the Apostle Islands.

Fishing is such a big part of Wisconsin life that it can cause arguments. For example, American Indians have the right to spear walleye and muskie on their old hunting grounds before the regular fishing seasons opens in spring. Some people claim the Indians take too many fish. In the past, the debate over traditional American Indian spearfishing became so heated that fights sometimes broke out as protesters tried to change Wisconsin's fishing laws.

In 1983, however, the federal courts ruled that under the treaties with the U.S. government, the Ojibwe tribe had the right to early spearfishing each spring. Biologists studying Wisconsin's lakes and streams also concluded that the fish population is healthy enough for everyone to get enough fish.

Fishing is a common pastime in the Badger State.

★ **American Birkebeiner Ski Race at Hayward**
Thousands of athletes glide across approximately 30 miles (50 km) of snow in February at the biggest cross-country ski race in North America.

★ **Summerfest in Milwaukee**
Big-name rock, pop, rhythm-and-blues, and country musicians perform along the shore of Lake Michigan during this eleven-day event beginning in late June.

★ **Great Circus Parade in Milwaukee**
Following tradition, each July, dozens of colorful horse-drawn wagons and hundreds of circus performers, along with elephants and other animals, snake through the streets of the city.

★ **Experimental Aircraft Association (EAA) AirVenture in Oshkosh**
Daredevil pilots tear up the sky at this July event, where experts show off thousands of historic and modern planes.

★ **Herbster Annual Smelt Fry**
Wisconsin fish fries are famous for their home-style food and warm hospitality. This one celebrates the smelt, a tasty little fish that swims upriver in April.

★ Honor the Earth Powwow in Hayward

American Indians from all around the Great Lakes region perform traditional ceremonies, songs, and dances at the Lac Courte Oreilles Ojibwe Reservation in July.

★ Brat Days in Sheboygan

The bratwurst, or "brat," is Wisconsin's most popular sausage. This feast, usually held in early August, serves it any number of ways, including on pizzas or in tacos.

★ Paavo Nurmi Marathon at Pence

Named for the famous Finnish runner, this August race is the state's oldest and most prestigious marathon. Treats for those who complete it include Finnish *mojakka* (stew).

★ Wisconsin State Fair in West Allis

Champion dairy cows, carnival rides, live entertainment, and hundreds of thousands of cream puffs are the focus of this August event.

★ Warrens Cranberry Festival

Each September, tiny Warrens hosts the world's biggest cranberry festival, featuring a big marching-band parade and hundreds of arts-and-crafts, antiques, and farm-products booths.

★ Green County Cheese Days

Watch an expert make cheese in a giant copper kettle at this Swiss-American festival in Monroe, held every two years in September.

★ Bayfield Apple Festival

Each October, apple farmers near Lake Superior celebrate the harvest by serving up all kinds of apple-filled treats, from pie and dumplings to sausage.

How the Government Works

The people of Wisconsin have a say in how the state grows and changes. They help run the Badger State by voting for leaders whose ideas they believe in and by sharing their own ideas. This is true both for local government—the governments of counties, cities, villages, and towns—and for the state government.

Local Government

Each county is governed by a group, or board, of officials called supervisors, elected by the people. Most city governments are headed by an elected mayor and council. Other cities have a council but no mayor. Instead, the elected council chooses a manager to run the city. Most villages are headed by an elected president and board of trustees. Instead of a president, some villages have a manager, who is picked by the board. Areas that do not belong to a city or a village are governed by a town government. Each town is headed by an elected board of supervisors.

Another unit of government is the school district, which runs the public schools. Wisconsin has more than 425 school districts, each governed by an elected board.

Every year, each town holds a meeting, at which citizens discuss and vote on important matters. Decisions made at the meeting then guide the work of the

The Wisconsin State Capitol is located in Madison.

Branches of Government

EXECUTIVE ★ ★ ★ ★ ★ ★ ★ ★ ★

The executive branch carries out the state's laws. It is headed by the governor. The governor suggests laws and starts programs that he or she thinks will benefit the state and appoints members of state boards and commissions. The governor is elected to a four-year term, as are the other chief members of the executive branch—the lieutenant governor, secretary of state, attorney general, treasurer, and state superintendent of public instruction.

LEGISLATIVE ★ ★ ★ ★ ★ ★ ★ ★

The Wisconsin legislature is divided into two houses: the senate, with thirty-three members, and the assembly, with ninety-nine members. Each senator serves a four-year term, while members of the assembly are elected for two years. The legislature develops, presents, and approves new laws.

JUDICIAL ★ ★ ★ ★ ★ ★ ★ ★

The highest court in Wisconsin is the state supreme court. Decisions made by lower courts can be appealed to the Wisconsin Supreme Court, which has seven justices, each elected to a ten-year term. Serving under the supreme court is the court of appeals, which mainly hears appeals from lower courts. Most cases are heard first by circuit courts. The judges of appellate and circuit courts are elected to six-year terms.

town supervisors. In addition, when officials in other types of local government are making an important decision, they often hold a public meeting at which citizens can voice their opinions.

State Government

Wisconsin's state government has three branches: executive, legislative, and judicial. The executive branch is headed by the governor. The legislative branch makes the state's laws. The judicial branch includes the state's courts. The legislature meets in the Wisconsin State Capitol, which also contains the governor's office, in Madison. Wisconsin's highest court, the supreme court, meets there as well.

How a Bill Becomes Law

Each member of the Wisconsin legislature represents the people of a certain district, or part of the state. Legislature members meet with citizens regularly to discuss whether to change old laws or create new laws. They write a draft, or bill, for every new law they propose.

Bills can be introduced in either the senate or the assembly in what is called a first reading. Usually a committee of senators or assembly members then studies the bill. The committee may hold a public hearing so that people outside the government can say what they think of the proposal. If the bill receives support in the committee, it usually goes back to the senate or assembly for a second reading. Members discuss the bill's good and bad points and may change, or amend, it.

When members have voted on all the amendments, the bill gets a third reading. Then the senate or assembly votes on it. If a majority of members vote in favor of the bill, it passes. Then it moves to the other

The legislative, executive, and judicial branches of the state government have chambers in the Wisconsin State Capitol.

WISCONSIN'S VOICE IN WASHINGTON

Wisconsinites also elect people to represent them in the U.S. Congress in Washington, D.C. The state has two members of the U.S. Senate, each elected by the state as a whole. As of 2010, Wisconsin had eight members of the U.S. House of Representatives, each elected from a separate district in the state.

house, where the same steps are repeated, except that the second house may skip the committee stage. Any amendments passed by one house have to also be approved by the other house.

Once both houses accept a bill, it goes to the governor, who can either allow it to become a law or reject it. The bill becomes a law if

Edwin Blashfield's mural "Resources of Wisconsin" decorates the ceiling of the Wisconsin State Capitol rotunda. It is the only granite dome in the United States.

the governor signs it or simply does not reject, or veto, it. Even if the governor vetoes the bill, it can still become law if two-thirds of each house again vote in favor of it.

Issues and Laws

One issued debated by Wisconsin citizens and lawmakers in recent years is protection of the state's landscape. As towns and cities have grown larger, farmlands have disappeared. Many citizens believe that cities should control the way they grow.

A law called the Smart Growth Initiative, which was passed by the senate and assembly and signed by the governor in 1999, says towns must carefully plan how they use the land around them. They must also make the most of the space they already have and conserve the state's woods, marshes, fields, and farms. Critics, however, worry that the law takes away rights from property owners and lets the state control local decisions about land use. In 2005, the governor vetoed an attempt by the legislature to repeal the law.

Wisconsin has also debated how best to take care of people who need public assistance. In 1997, it started Wisconsin Works, a job-training and employment program for the poor. The idea behind Wisconsin Works, or W-2, is that the government should help jobless people to find work instead of just giving them money. The goal is to help citizens become independent.

When W-2 was created, it was admired so much that it became a model for a national program. The number of people getting state aid dropped by 50 percent between 1997 and 2000. But critics worried that some people might not be getting enough help from W-2. A new state agency set up in 2008—the Department of Children and Families—oversees the W-2 program to improve services for families needing assistance.

Unemployed paper-mill workers attend a job-searching seminar at the city hall in Park Falls.

Joining the Action

If you want to support an idea you believe in, there are many ways to get involved. One step is to write a letter or send an e-mail to a state leader. You can write to the governor, for example, or to your representatives in the legislature. Another way to make your voice heard is by joining a club or organization that supports the same causes you do. A group often has more power than an individual. When people team up, they are difficult to ignore.

It is also good to read newspapers (in print or online) and get news from the radio or television or the websites of TV news organizations, so that you can keep up-to-date on what is happening in your

A bicyclist wears a "One Less Car" sign on his back during a demonstration at the Wisconsin State Capitol in Madison.

state. Since 2007, Wisconsinites have had an easy way to get a more complete and close-up look at their state government in action. The private network WisconsinEye, broadcasting on television and the Internet, covers proceedings in all three branches.

Making a Living

When Europeans first came to what is now Wisconsin, they found a land full of promise. Green forests offered timber for building. The south and the west were blessed with rich soil. The region also had plenty of water, from its thousands of lakes, rivers, and streams to its major waterways—Lakes Michigan and Superior and the Mississippi River. Over the years, these natural resources have more than lived up to their powerful potential. People have used them to build booming industries that have become the backbone of Wisconsin's strong economy.

America's Dairyland

Take a drive across the southern part of the state, from Prairie du Chien to Milwaukee, and one sight will soon become familiar: black-and-white spotted cows grazing peacefully on green pastures. Wisconsin's 1.25 million dairy cows produced more than 24 billion pounds (11 billion kg) of milk in 2008. Its factories make one-fourth of the nation's cheese and about one-fifth of its butter. Thousands of tons of dried and evaporated milk and millions of gallons of ice cream are made in the state, too. It is no wonder Wisconsin is known as America's Dairyland.

About half of Wisconsin's farm income comes from its dairy products. Another large portion is earned selling chickens, eggs, beef cattle, and hogs.

Wisconsin is home to thousands of dairy farms, including this one near Delavan.

Quick Facts

COW OFFICIALLY NUMBER ONE

The dairy cow is the state's official domestic animal. Wisconsin has many different breeds, or types, of cows. Each year the secretary of the Department of Agriculture, Trade, and Consumer Protection chooses one of these types to be the year's official breed.

Wisconsin farmers also grow corn, which is the official state grain, as well as hay, soybeans, winter wheat, mint, and tobacco. They are among the country's top producers of vegetables for canning, including green peas, snap beans, sweet corn, and cabbage for sauerkraut.

A twelve-year-old milks a cow on his grandfather's farm. The family milks more than one hundred dairy cattle a day.

This Wisconsin farm grows corn, which was chosen as the state's official grain in 1989.

Wisconsin leads the country in the production of cranberries, which grow in the marshy soil of the Central Sands and in several northern counties. Orchards in Door and Kewaunee counties supply the Midwest with apples and tart cherries.

Today Wisconsin has far fewer farms than it did a hundred years ago, but the farms that survive are much larger. Together they cover almost half the land.

Workers & Industries

Industry	Number of People Working in That Industry	Percentage of All Workers Who Are Working in That Industry
Education and health care	603,799	21.0%
Manufacturing	558,062	19.4%
Wholesale and retail businesses	421,693	14.7%
Publishing, media, entertainment, hotels, and restaurants	288,077	10.0%
Professionals, scientists, and managers	214,951	7.5%
Banking and finance, insurance, and real estate	189,945	6.6%
Construction	180,215	6.3%
Transportation and public utilities	136,549	4.7%
Other services	112,775	3.9%
Government	96,467	3.4%
Farming, fishing, forestry, and mining	72,508	2.5%
Totals	**2,875,041**	**100%**

Notes: Figures above do not include people in the armed forces. "Professionals" includes people such as doctors and lawyers. Percentages may not add to 100 because of rounding.

Source: U.S. Bureau of the Census, 2007 estimates

Manufacturing

Agriculture has always been an important part of the Wisconsin economy, but manufacturing has made the state grow and prosper. Huge paper mills near Green Bay and in the Fox River Valley produce everything from tissues to typing paper. Factories in the Milwaukee area make X-ray machines and other medical equipment, engines and turbines, power cranes, farm equipment, knives, and other metal tools. One well-known Milwaukee business, the Harley-Davidson Motor Company, has been making motorcycles since 1903.

Food processing plays a major role in Wisconsin's economy, too. Creameries and cheese factories dot the state, and Lakeside Foods, one of the largest vegetable canners in the country, is based in Manitowoc. Food-processing plants in Rock County make snack foods such as potato chips and corn chips. Given Wisconsin's strong German heritage, it is no surprise that the state is also home to a successful sausage industry.

Quick Facts

KLEENEX
Kimberly-Clark, a paper company founded in Neenah, created the world's first disposable handkerchiefs in 1924. These delicate tissues, once known as Cellu-wipes, were originally marketed as makeup removers. They were later renamed Kleenex Kerchiefs.

A foundry worker operates a metal saw in a Wisconsin factory.

Milwaukee has been known as the beer capital of the United States. It had almost 160 breweries by the time of the Civil War. Milwaukee was once home to the giant Schlitz, Pabst, and Miller breweries. But by 2000, only Miller remained as the city's beer powerhouse. Wisconsin today has dozens of microbreweries—companies that make gourmet beer in small batches.

Tourism

Wisconsin is one of the Midwest's most popular vacation places, and more than $7 billion of the state's income comes from tourism each year. Visitors love to fish its lakes and streams and sunbathe on the sandy beaches of Lake Michigan. In winter, thousands of miles of snowmobile trails attract adventurers.

Tourists also come to see Wisconsin's unique architecture. Twentieth-century architect Frank Lloyd Wright's elegant buildings are scattered across the state.

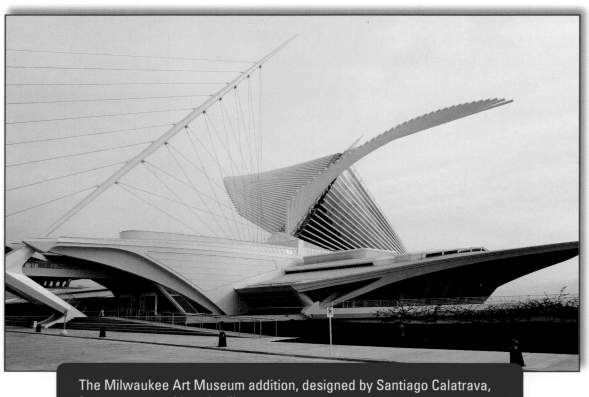

The Milwaukee Art Museum addition, designed by Santiago Calatrava, features a movable, winglike sunscreen.

Even more spectacular is the Quadracci Pavilion of the Milwaukee Art Museum. Set on the shore of Lake Michigan, this graceful structure of steel, glass, and white concrete, designed by Spanish architect Santiago Calatrava, looks like a bird about to take flight. Completed in 2001 at a cost of more than $100 million, the pavilion is famous around the world.

Wisconsin's Indian reservations and casinos are another big tourist attraction. Like most states, Wisconsin forbids gambling. But in 1988, Congress passed a law stating that such rules do not apply on Indian lands. Since then, many Wisconsin tribes have built casinos in an effort to earn money. On many reservations, more people work in gaming than in any other business, and the hotels and restaurants that surround the casinos have created even more jobs. As a result, the population on reservations is rising.

Milwaukee's Potawatomi Bingo Casino opened in 1991.

Products & Resources

Dairy Farms

With more than 13,000 dairy farms, Wisconsin is a leading producer of milk, butter, and cheese. The largest grouping of dairy cows is in the area between Green Bay and Monroe.

Cranberries

The cranberry is the state fruit. Roughly half of the nation's cranberries are grown in Wisconsin.

Paper

Wisconsin makes more paper than any other state. Its gigantic mills create wood pulp from trees such as pine, poplar, spruce, and hemlock.

Machinery

The Badger State is a major producer of heavy machinery. These products include turbines, tractors, and construction equipment.

Education

Wisconsin takes pride in its well-respected educational institutions. The University of Wisconsin system, one of the largest state university systems in the country, includes thirteen four-year colleges, an equal number of two-year colleges, and a total of 175,000 students. The main campus of the University of Wisconsin, at Madison, widely considered one of the best public universities in the country, is a leader in science and technology research. The state is also home to leading private schools of higher education, such as Marquette and Lawrence universities and Beloit College.

Waterways

Wisconsin ships goods around the world from its Great Lakes ports. Its 15,000 inland lakes and more than 10,000 miles (16,000 km) of trout streams, as well as its Great Lakes shorelines, help keep its tourist industry strong as well.

Protecting the Land

Wisconsinites want their state to have a strong economy, but not at the expense of the state's natural resources and beauty. Industries such as manufacturing, tourism, and even farming can put a heavy burden on the environment and the natural resources that keep the economy alive. A big challenge that faces the state today is protecting its most plentiful resource—water.

Water pollution has threatened Wisconsin for more than a century. Paper mills were once some of the state's worst polluters. They dumped tons of harmful chemicals into rivers and lakes, causing fish to die. In the 1960s, laws

Wisconsinites value their state's lakes and streams.

were passed that required companies to control their waste. As a result, the waters around the factories and centers of industry are much cleaner.

A bigger worry these days is a problem called nonpoint source pollution. Many of the unhealthy chemicals that find their way into Wisconsin's water do not come from a single place such as a factory. Instead, they come from a variety of sources, such as farmers who spread pesticides, cars that drip motor oil, and construction workers who use tar to repair roads. As rain or melted snow flows across fields, driveways, and highways, it picks up these poisons and carries them along until they reach streams, rivers, lakes, and wetlands.

Almost half of Wisconsin's streams and 90 percent of its inland lakes are threatened by nonpoint source pollution. The results can be deadly. In 1993, a tiny organism called *Cryptosporidium* got into Milwaukee's drinking water.

In Their Own Words

Conservation is a state of harmony between men and land. . . . Harmony with land is like harmony with a friend; you cannot cherish his right hand and chop off his left.

—Wisconsin conservationist Aldo Leopold

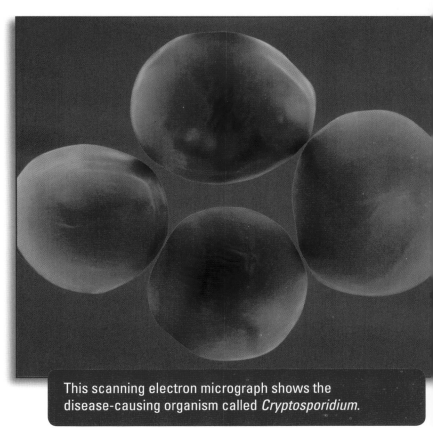

This scanning electron micrograph shows the disease-causing organism called *Cryptosporidium*.

Residents and businesses can help reduce polluted runoff from roads and roofs by planting rain gardens. Native plantings capture rainwater that filters slowly into the ground instead of running off into storm sewers.

As a result, about 400,000 people got sick, and dozens died. Scientists think the "bug" was probably carried from fields full of cow manure.

The state now purifies, or cleans, its water more carefully. But to keep new poisons from turning up, it is focusing on prevention, too. The government is helping farmers switch to new methods that keep animal waste and chemicals from being washed away. Planting grass along waterways, for example, helps trap particles in the soil.

Wherever you live, you and your family can help by using natural fertilizers. You can keep the ground free of pet waste. You can also plant bushes, trees, and other plants to soak up the rain—such as in a well-planned rain garden.

State Flag & Seal

The state flag has a blue background with the state coat of arms in the center. Above the coat of arms is the state's name, and below it, the year of statehood. The coat of arms shows a large shield held by a sailor and a miner, who represent labor on water and on land. The shield bears symbols that stand for agriculture, mining, manufacturing, and shipping. To show loyalty to the country, the middle of the shield has the U.S. coat of arms. Below the shield are a horn of plenty and a pyramid of thirteen pieces of lead. The horn of plenty represents prosperity and abundance. The pyramid stands for mineral wealth and also for the thirteen original U.S. states. Above the shield is the state animal, the badger, along with a banner that carries Wisconsin's motto, "Forward."

The state seal shows the Wisconsin coat of arms along with the words "Great Seal of the State of Wisconsin." A curved line of thirteen stars lies below the coat of arms. It stands for the thirteen original U.S. states. The seal is round and has a sawtooth edge.

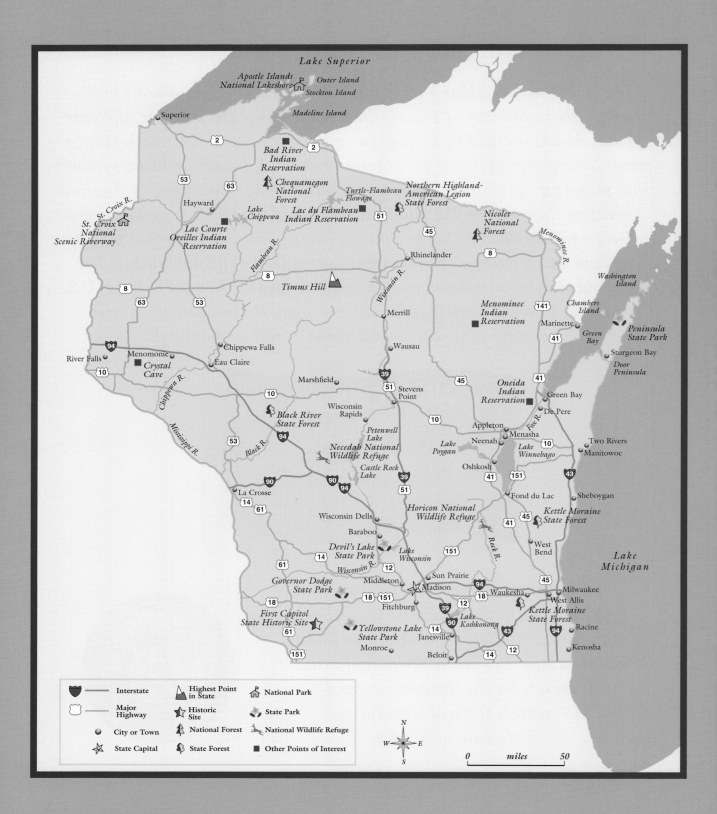

Lake Superior

Apostle Islands
National Lakeshore
Outer Island
Stockton Island

Madeline Island

Superior

2

2

Bad River
Indian
Reservation

53

63

Chequamegon
National
Forest

Turtle-Flambeau
Flowage

Northern Highland-
American Legion
State Forest

Hayward

Lake
Chippewa

Lac du Flambeau
Indian Reservation

51

Nicolet
National
Forest

St. Croix R.

St. Croix
National
Scenic Riverway

Lac Courte
Oreilles Indian
Reservation

Flambeau R.

45

8

Menominee R.

Rhinelander

8

Washington
Island

8

Timms Hill

Menominee
Indian
Reservation

141

Chambers
Island

63

53

Merrill

Wisconsin R.

Marinette

Green
Bay

Peninsula
State Park

94

Wausau

45

41

Sturgeon Bay

River Falls

Menomonie
Crystal
Cave

Chippewa Falls

Eau Claire

Marshfield

39

Oneida
Indian
Reservation

41

Green Bay

Door
Peninsula

10

10

Chippewa R.

51

Stevens
Point

45

De Pere

Two Rivers

Mississippi R.

53

Black R.

Black River
State Forest

94

Wisconsin
Rapids

10

Appleton

Neenah
Menasha

Manitowoc

Fox R.

10

Petenwell
Lake

Necedah National
Wildlife Refuge

Lake
Poygan

90

90

94

Castle Rock
Lake

39

51

Oshkosh

41

151

Lake
Winnebago

43

Sheboygan

La Crosse

14

61

Wisconsin Dells

Baraboo

Horicon National
Wildlife Refuge

Fond du Lac

Kettle Moraine
State Forest

West
Bend

Lake
Michigan

61

14

Devil's Lake
State Park

Lake
Wisconsin

151

Rock R.

41

45

Governor Dodge
State Park

Wisconsin R.

12

Middleton

Sun Prairie

Madison

Milwaukee

18

First Capitol
State Historic Site

18

151

Fitchburg

39

12

94

Waukesha

45

West Allis

18

Kettle Moraine
State Forest

61

Yellowstone Lake
State Park

14

90

Lake
Koshkonong

43

94

Racine

Monroe

Janesville

Kenosha

151

Beloit

14

12

Interstate

Highest Point
in State

National Park

Major
Highway

Historic
Site

State Park

City or Town

National Forest

National Wildlife Refuge

State Capital

State Forest

Other Points of Interest

N

W   E

S

0   miles   50

76 WISCONSIN

State Song

"On, Wisconsin!"

words by J. S. Hubbard and C. D. Rosa
music by William T. Purdy

★ MORE ABOUT WISCONSIN ★

BOOKS

Fandel, Jennifer. *Frank Lloyd Wright*. Mankato, MN: Creative Education, 2006.

Holliday, Diane, and Bobbie Malone. *Digging and Discovery: Wisconsin Archaeology*. Madison, WI: Wisconsin Historical Society, 2006.

Kasparek, Jonathan. *Voices and Votes: How Democracy Works in Wisconsin*. Madison, WI: Wisconsin Historical Society, 2006.

Porter, Adele. *Wild About Wisconsin Birds: A Youth's Guide to the Birds of Wisconsin*. Cambridge, MN: Adventure Publications, 2009.

Poulakidas, Georgene. *Black Hawk's War*. New York: PowerKids Press/Primary Source, 2006.

Stone, Tanya Lee. *Laura Ingalls Wilder*. New York: DK, 2009.

Wyckoff, Edwin Brit. *Electric Guitar Man: The Genius of Les Paul*. Berkeley Heights, NJ: Enslow Publishers, 2008.

WEBSITES

State of Wisconsin:
http://www.wisconsin.gov

Wisconsin Department of Natural Resources: EEK! Environmental Education for Kids:
http://www.dnr.state.wi.us/org/caer/ce/eek

Wisconsin Department of Tourism:
http://www.travelwisconsin.com

Margaret Dornfeld is a writer, editor, and translator. She likes to travel to Milwaukee to visit family, explore old neighborhoods, and enjoy the city's German cuisine. Dornfeld's German ancestors settled in Lebanon, Wisconsin, around 1850.

Richard Hantula and his family come from the Gogebic Range of Wisconsin and Michigan. Now based in New York, Hantula has worked as a writer and editor for more than three decades.

Page numbers in **boldface** are illustrations.